COVER
DESIGN LAYOUT
HALİL SÖNMEZ

Original Turkish writting and page design by
Halil Sonmez

Turkish to English Translation by
Aydin Yulug

Library of Congress Num. 1224381

ISBN: 1-59971-706-9

2

INTRODUCTION

My poem named "Indefinitely" is based on postmodernism expressions and consists of two different sections: poemism and postpoemism.

I have called the first section "poemism", which is derived from modernism.

The interpersonal relationships changes from the past to the current time, its causal relationship with the philosophical world; the societal family's.

Postmodernist abilities and the subject of the postmodernism philosophy is an abstract map:

The global financial sea that is constantly enlarging,

a separation from the whole within the new pluralistic scenario.

The actual abstract universality that is experienced and the cause of this abstract universality,

Postmodernism, and its internal organization

Defining the behavioral limits of the society

And finally, the god of spaces that has been defined by postmodernist authors

in societal analysis books
with totalistic reasoning.
In the second section, postpoemism,
with a name derived from postmodernism
and meaning the aftermath of the poem's
formation.
The poem starts from the middle and, in a
way that destroys totalistic reasoning,
flow with poet and nut man figures with
abbreviations that may be figures or
inventions and potpourri transitions.
Without a definite start point.
It ends with its subject within the text
in a way that shows 'art for art's sake'.
All this study emphasizes the role
of internal migration, and simulates
the loss of meaning in the media and the
social life in the masses.

HALIL SONMEZ

Indefinitely

6-18-07

Halil Sonmez born in Adana,Turkey in 03/11/71

J@ AD- ALMY. HEART
ENJOY. Riece-

HALIL SONMEZ

Poetrysm

You let them soon to happen,
Indefinetly.
your inquiries, the answer to questions,
in every corner of the Earth
a new complex of changes.
Seeing you,
did not resolve you.

POEM:

In a place like the world, seeing
the human content
is empty within itself .
Devoid of dreams,
interacting with nature,
in its past,
with all its objects.
An entity onto itself.
Lover of dreams and sciences,
impressionist.
Observe this living moment,
a new pluralistic period was conditioned
for the transition of the new.
Not in reality;
in a value present in the dreams world.

POEM:

So much,
you were disconnected, just like that.
From dream to dream,
depriving the man
from certainty.

So much ,
were you, a product of consciousness,
just like that,
in the middle of a trembling,
subject get separated from object .

POEM:

So much,
out of yourself,
you were the object itself ,
just like that ,
Traveling on a rootless track.

POEM:

Is watching
       because of
              walking.

Is walking
       because of
              watching.

All a chaos !

POEM:

So much,
were you , an emptiness , just like that ,
where the soul solidified ,
extending its boundaries

So close,
So much indefinite, just like that.

In man
        In between
                Like space

POEM:

I have been watching you.
I don't get your shape.
I can't love you
with the gravities of love.
Like the lunatic, with absolutely no role in
life,
To whom I love,
I love you like that.
Among the crowd
being by yourself was a sign for everyone,
so indefinite,
so close.
To live this being you
irritates.
Brings science to its feet
to try
the atoms on assumptions.

POEM:

Trying
Quantifies
This pluralistic love.
Emphasizes failure.
No entity behind
Or in front
Play together.
The now of the moment
Starts where it finishes.
The rare coincidence
Living
Stops with a risk.
Such as to be or not to be.

POEM:

So much,
Were you on and off,
Just like that.
Coming with the now of the moment.

So much,
out of yourself,
you were the object itself ,
just like that ,
Traveling on a rootless track.

POEM:

So much,
Were you a product of consciousness,
Just like that.
Where the soul solidified,
Extending its boundaries.

So much indeterminate,
So close,
Just like that .

Outside
  Within the
      Majority

POEM:

I take and leave,
From the chambers of my brain.
It was a coincidence on the world's side
streets,
of the blocks residents,
where you were just someone.
To talk,
In verb conjugations,
Pictured what you said,
Without a dream.
The artists',
Brushstrokes were where I found,
How you could not be found.

POEM:

Slow light,
Your eyes moved,
On lines.
You merged reality and dream,
In case it would look like something.

POEM:

You became an object,
Of its maybe.
You lived,
You did not live.
In the poem,
That the You had written as it wished.
The symbol where the picture is present,
But there is no dream,
That you thought,
And multiplied like the other.

In the brushstrokes
    Of
        Painters

POEM:

A new us was being born.
We talked of what we did not know,
When we came together.
Just like,
The objects.
Image reflected from afar.
In our perspective closeness,
With abstract numbers,
We subtracted and added,
Each other.
In the first point scale,
I could see your ambiguity,
As though it had started from somewhere.
In sheets continuously doodled,
By lunatics,
You showed one with a name.
The other with a verb.
Like a subject,
Like a piece of timelessness.

POEM:

It finished and started,
Our mental story's,
Poetic existence.
With every image of culture.
Poetic,
We played,
And sang the harmony.
Once upon a time,
Between commas,
Of being by yourself.

POEM:

See once again,
The land, the waters, the seas.
Sense
In the smell of ozone,
The rose droplet rains.
Touch,
Blooming everywhere in every color,
Roses every sequence an atom.
Hold in its light,
With your eyes,
The moon and the sun,
The sky, the stars.
Travel all the planets.
Think,
In the sense that it was there,
The dust particle universe.

POEM:

It was living right or wrong.
The reality,
Due to its flow to each other.
Love like photosynthesis dreams,
Science on one side.
Will find us in lost matters,
Sees two abstract realities,
In third worlds.
The other that multiplies with you.

POEM:

See in your dreams,
The rising slow light movement,
Drawing with its duration,
Unlimited opening and creating,
Thin endless space.
Definite,
All subconsciously timed,
Appears to those that appear.
Converted,
Into a lunatic restrainer,
It's being by itself.

POEM:

Passes from our time,
The transition to each other,
The coincidence of everything,
The reality.
Passes through our knowledge,
The abstract universality,
With all its desire,
That is within,
The dream within.

POEM:

So a new day has been born.
I have woken up.
So it is evening now.
I have gone home.
So I am thinking.
You, me, us, you, them,
Her.
Meaning she was there.
Living place, same procedure,
Returning to the same place.
The utilitarian discipline,
Within the rational flow.
X's,
Like she,

POEM:

So I am thinking,
Returning,
To the same place.
Living place, same procedure.
The utilitarian discipline,
Within the rational flow

POEM:

So a new day has been born.
I have woken up.
So it is evening now.
I have gone home.
So I am thinking,
With the object of my thought.
I am at the same place,
Meaning she was there.
We were returning to the same place.
The utilitarian discipline,
Within the rational flow.
Separate
　　Detaching
　　Detaching
　　Detaching

POEM:

Lots of
    Returning
        Detaching
            Detaching
                Detaching

Lots of,
Living the same thing.
Lots of,
Not remembering with something else.
The new one,
Multiplying so many times.
Getting smaller,
Spreading so many times.
Close and far places,
Growing so many times.
Returning to the same place,
Its an historical story.

POEM:

Once upon a time,
Your stays were decreasing,
As though no memory would be left.
The clouds are moving away,
From your skin.
The color was fading,
From your eyes more beautiful than green.

POEM:

So much
Were you a dream just like that
From disconnection to disconnection
Depriving a man
From certainty

So much
Were you remembrance just like that
Chasing the same philosophy
With every variation

POEM:

With pleasure,
Of everything.
Each new different world,
Each new love,
Together with friendship,
In probability, in praise, in judgment,
Turns to face itself.
Living,
Should remind.

POEM:

Your completely naked existence's,
Noise buzzing in everything.
Life draws,
A broken,
Surrealist track for it.
Even when the bird is the tree branch,
And the sky its wings,
Floating in the blue,
Does not care,
Freedom should not be broken.

POEM:

I am writing

The name of
      God
          As you destroyed it.
In a postmodern world.

POEM:

Your completely naked freedom ,
Noise buzzing,
In everything.
I'm a poet.
It passes through my dreams,
Your life,
When the wind combs your hair.
The reality of being a God,
Like a lover's dream.
Freedom.

POEM:

One searches,
For your soul in the travel logbook.
Sand verses write your name,
When deleted by the sea's hands.
I am the one that is destroyed,
Her soul,
Lost, complex.
In abstract cities,
Far away.
Her image.

POEM:

You let them soon to happen,
indefinitely.
A God like you
The God of empty spaces
So much
Everything you were just like that
One that, in every situation,
Created events

POEM:

So much,
were you , an emptiness , just like that ,
where the soul solidified ,
extending its boundaries

So much
Were you on and off
Just like that
Coming with the now of the moment

POEM:

So much ,
Were you, a product of consciousness,
Just like that,
Trembling the moment,
The subject is separated from the object.

So much, out of yourself,
you were the object itself ,
just like that,
Traveling on a rootless track.

POEM:

Postpoemism

POEM:

Is watching

> Because of
>> walking.

Is walking

> Because of

>> Watching.

All a chaos!

Poet:

The   Nut Man:

POEM:

A new us was being born.
We talked of what we did not know,
When we came together.
Just like,
The objects.
Image reflected from afar.
In our perspective closeness,
With abstract numbers,
We subtracted and added,
Each other.
In the first point scale,
I could see your ambiguity,
As though it had started from somewhere.
In sheets continuously doodled by lunatics,
You showed one with a name, the other with
a verb,
Like a subject, like a piece of timelessness.

Poet:

The Nut Man:

POEM:

So a new day has been born.
I have woken up.
So it is evening now.
I have gone home.
So I am thinking.
You, me, us, you, them,
Her.
Meaning she was there.
Living place, same procedure,
Returning to the same place.
The utilitarian discipline,
Within the rational flow.
X's,
Like O .

Poet:

The Nut Man:

POEM:

I take and leave,
From the chambers of my brain.
On the world's side streets,
Of the street residents,
Were you just one of.
To talk,
In verb conjugations.
Pictured what you said,
Without a dream.
The artists',
Brushstrokes were where I found,
How you could not be found.
Outside
 Within the
   Majority.

Poet:

The Nut Man:

POEM:

I being watching you.
I don get your shape.
I can't love you
with the gravities of love.
Like the lunatic, with absolutely no role in
life,
To whom I love,
I love you like that.
Among the crowd
being by yourself was a sign for everyone,
so indefinite,
so close.
To live this being you
irritates.
Brings science to its feet
to try
the atoms on assumptions.

Poet:

The Nut Man:

POEM:

Trying,
Quantifies,
This pluralistic love.
Emphasizes failure.
No entity behind,
Or in front,
Play together.
The now of the moment,
Starts where it finishes.
The rare coincidence.
Living,
Stops with a risk,
Such as to be or not to be.

Poet:

The Nut Man:

POEM:

You became an object,
Of its maybe.
You lived,
You did not live.
In the poem,
That the You had written as it wished.
The symbol where the picture is present,
But there is no dream,
That you thought,
And multiplied like the other.

In the brushstrokes
        Of
                Painters

Poet:

The Nut Man:

POEM:

See in your dreams,
The rising slow light movement.
Drawing with its duration,
Unlimited opening and creating,
Thin endless space.
Definite,
All subconsciously timed.
Appears to those that appear,
Converted,
Into a lunatic restrainer.
It's being by itself.

Poet:

The Nut Man:

POEM:

Passes from our time,
The transition to each other,
The coincidence of everything,
The reality.
Passes through our knowledge,
The abstract universality,
With all its desire,
That is within,
The dream within.

Poet:

The Nut Man:

POEM:

So a new day has been born.
I have woken up.
So it is evening now.
I have gone home.
So I am thinking,
With the object of my thought.
I am at the same place,
Meaning she was there.
We were returning to the same place .
The utilitarian discipline,
Within the rational flow.

Poet:

The Nut Man:

POEM:

A new us was being born.
We talked of what we did not know,
When we came together.
Just like,
The objects.
Image reflected from afar,
In our perspective closeness.
Separate
 Returning.
The bird
          The branch.
Detaching
          Turning

Such as to be or not to be.

Poet:

The Nut Man:

POEM:

With pleasure each new,
Different world,
Multiplying so many times.
Getting smaller,
Spreading so many times.
Trying,
The atoms on assumptions.
Growing so many times.
The distant place and the near.
I'm a poet,
It passes through my dreams,
In abstract cities.

Poet:

The Nut Man:

You let them soon to happen,
indefinitely.

Poet:

The Nut Man:

POEM:

Not in reality

In the world of dreams

In value

You became an object ,
Of its maybe.
You lived and You did not live,
In the poem,
That the You had written as it wished.
The symbol where the picture is present,
But there is no dream.
That you thought,
And multiplied like the other.

99

Poet:

The Nut Man:

POEM:

As though it had started from somewhere.
In pieces of paper,
Doodled on continuously by nuts.
Slow light,
Your eyes moved,
On lines.
You merged reality and dream,
In case it would look like,
Something.

Poet:

The Nut Man:

POEM:

See in your dreams,
The rising,
slow light movement,
Drawing with its duration,
Unlimited opening and creating,
Thin endless space.
Definite.
A new us,
was being born.
We talked of
what we did not know
When we came together.
Just like
The objects,
Image reflected,
from afar,
In our perspective closeness.

Poet:

The Nut Man:

POEM:

It finished and started,
Our mental story's,
Poetic existence.
With every image of culture.
Poetic.

We played and sang
The harmony
So I am thinking
Returning to the same place
Living place same procedure
Meaning she was there
X's like O

105

Poet:

The Nut Man:

POEM:

I take and leave,
From the chambers of my brain.
On the world's side streets,
Of the street residents,
Were you just one of.
To talk,
In verb conjugations.
Pictured what you said,
Without a dream.

Poet:

The Nut Man:

POEM:

I being watching you.
I don get your shape.
I can't love you
with the gravities of love.
Like the lunatic, with absolutely no role in
life,
To whom I love,
I love you like that.
Among the crowd
being by yourself was a sign for everyone,
so indefinite,
so close.
To live this being you
irritates.
Brings science to its feet.

Poet:

The Nut Man:

POEM:

With pleasure,
Each new different world,
Multiplying so many times,
Getting smaller.
Spreading so many times,
The distant place and the near,
In abstract cities.

Poet:

The Nut Man:

You let them soon to happen,
 indefinitely.

Poet:

The Nut Man:

Poet:
    you
       me
          us

    you
       them
          her
Meaning she was there
I being watching you.
I don get your shape.
I can't love you
with the gravities of love.
So indefinite,
So close

The Nut Man:

So much,
were you, an emptiness, just like that,
In man
      In between
          Like space

Poet:

It was living right or wrong.
The reality,
Due to its flow to each other.
Love like photosynthesis dreams,
Science on one side.
Finds us in lost places.
Sees two abstract realities,
In third worlds.

The Nut Man:

So much
Were you remembrance just like that
Chasing the same philosophy
With every difference

Poet:

Once upon a time
Your stays were decreasing.
As though no memory would be left.
The clouds are moving away,
From your skin

The Nut Man:

You have fallen so much just like that
In the brushstrokes
    Of
    Painters

Poet:

With abstract numbers,
We subtracted and added,
Each other.
In the first point scale
I could see your ambiguity
As though it had started from somewhere.
In pieces of paper,
Doodled constantly by lunatics,
You showed one with a name,
And the other with a verb.

The Nut Man:

So much were you a product of
consciousness
Just like that
Outside
Within the
  Majority

Poet:

Each new different world
Together in probability.
Close and far places.
I'm a poet
It passes through my dreams.

The Nut Man:

Indefinitely

EVEN IF ONLY PARTIALLY

I see postmodernism as the delaying of
reality
In the period of modernism.
In our lives
Having things that are indeterminate and
close to us
Are interactions developing
Within a postmodern behavior or its
esthetics.
The interactions that are difficult to cross
By delaying them lead to confusion in
people living today
And, as a small example, resort to using the
law more often
The best way to protect yourself and others
in this matter
Will be to remember.

COLLECTED BY
Halil Sonmez

1997 Turkey /Adana - 2005 USA /New York